MW00399434

FR. MARK TOUPS

In Saint Joseph's Footsteps

30 DAYS OF MEDITATIONS

ASCENSION

West Chester, Pennsylvania

Fr. Mark Toups is a priest of the Diocese of Houma-Thibodaux, where he serves as vicar general and the pastor of Our Lady of the Isle Church in Grand Isle, Louisiana. He is also an adjunct faculty member at the Institute for Priestly Formation. Fr. Toups is the author of *Oremus: A Catholic Guide to Prayer*, the *Rejoice! Advent Meditation* sseries, *The Ascension Lenten Companion* series, and *The Way of the Cross: Praying the Psalms with Jesus*.

Nihil obstat:	Rev. S. Brice Higginbotham
	Censor librorum
	May 7, 2021
Imprimatur:	Most Rev. Shelton J. Fabre
	Bishop of Houma-Thibodaux
	May 7, 2021

The *nihil obstat* and *imprimatur* are official declarations that a book or pamphlet is free of doctrinal or moral error. No implication is contained therein that those who have granted the *nihil obstat* or *imprimatur* agree with the content, opinion, or statements expressed.

Ascension, PO Box 1990, West Chester, PA 19380
1-800-376-0520 • ascensionpress.com

Cover design: Rosemary Strohm
Printed in the United States of America
21 22 23 24 25 5 4 3 2 1
ISBN 978-1-950784-88-2 (paperback)
ISBN 978-1-950784-89-9 (ebook)

*I dedicate this book to the memory of
Msgr. Bill Fitzgerald and Canon Digby Samuels.
These men "were" Joseph.
Fitz and Digby, pray for us*

CONTENTS

PREFACE

I first *saw* St. Joseph when I was a kid. There are statues of him in every Catholic church in South Louisiana—and there are a lot of Catholic churches in Cajun Country. Each statue looked the same. Joseph was older, holding Jesus in his arms and holding a white lily. To a young boy who was wild at heart, those statues looked effeminate, and neither his age nor that lily appealed to me. For much of my life I kept Joseph at a distance, because I had nothing in common with the statue.

I first *discovered* Joseph through the Institute for Priestly Formation (IPF). IPF's mission is to form seminarians, priests, and bishops in holiness and accompany them in their ongoing spiritual growth so that they can more effectively lead others to Christ. There, I started to learn about who St. Joseph really is, often through conversations with IPF priests—priests like Msgr. Bill Fitzgerald, who embodied St. Joseph and inspired me to learn more about him.

I first *met* Joseph when I began to write the *Rejoice! Advent Meditations* series. As each year in the series progressed, St. Joseph's presence became more personal for me. I sought his intercession, began to experience his presence in prayer, and learned in contemplation what books couldn't teach me.

In my humble opinion, St. Joseph may be the most underestimated saint in history. He may also be the most misunderstood saint in history. Far from an effeminate man holding a lily, Joseph was a *man*. He was hand-picked from all the men in history to act as an agent of God the Father, revealing both masculinity and fatherhood to Jesus Christ. He was a spiritual giant who taught Jesus how to pray. He was a fierce protector who led his family to Egypt to safeguard the life of the baby entrusted to him. He also conquered himself to protect the purity of the Virgin Mary and so allowed her to feel safer with him than anywhere in the world. Joseph was a man. He was a dad. He was a saint.

On December 8, 2020, Pope Francis dedicated the coming year to St. Joseph. After rejoicing in the Holy Father's announcement, I asked the Lord, as well as St. Joseph, if there was anything that I might do in celebration of the year that would honor Joseph and help others get to know him. *In St. Joseph's Footsteps: Thirty Days of Meditations* is a direct response to what I felt the Lord asking me to do.

Thanks be to God, there are resources that help us learn about St. Joseph and consecrate ourselves to Jesus through him. It is my hope that *In St. Joseph's Footsteps* will help you get to know the person of St. Joseph on a personal level, in your heart.

The guided meditations here are not meant to replace your prayer but to help you enter into an encounter. In them I ask to visualize what it might have been like to be Joseph in various moments in his life. At the end of each mediation is a short spiritual exercise. Here I invite you to read and pray with the Scripture verses associated with each meditation and provide a few lines in case you want to write anything down.

It is my hope that the simple words of this book will help you pray, so that there, in contemplation, St. Joseph might teach you just as he taught Jesus.

Enjoy the meditations. Enjoy getting to know Joseph.

BETROTHAL

Joseph is first mentioned in the Bible in the first chapters of both Matthew and Luke. In both Gospels, our introduction to Joseph mentions that he was betrothed to Mary.

In ancient Israel, marriage was a two-part process. First came the rite of betrothal, a formal and public ceremony that included the exchange of vows. The betrothal lasted about a year. During this time, the couple were considered married in each other's eyes and in the eyes of the community, but the woman remained with her parents and the man prepared a home for his wife. At the end of the betrothal, a wedding ceremony took place, this one much grander than the first, often lasting up to seven days. Now the husband brought his wife into their home, and the marriage was consummated.

When we first meet Joseph in Matthew's Gospel, we read that he is betrothed to Mary, his wife. Our journey with Joseph begins here, with his betrothal, and all that occurs during this time in his life.

Day 1
PSALMS

Joseph was a man of profound holiness. Prayer was a way of life, not merely something he did once or only twice a day. As oxygen was to his body, so were the psalms the "oxygen" for his prayer. As we imagine a day in the life of Joseph, let us ask the Holy Spirit to help us imagine Joseph as a man of prayer, a man of the psalms.

Let us imagine Joseph as he wakes from sleep and opens his eyes. The first words from his mouth are the same words that he has spoken every morning since his childhood: "O LORD, open my lips, and my mouth shall show forth your praise" (Psalm 51:15). He soon sits upright in his bed and slowly whispers a prayer consecrating the day to the Lord, concluding as he says aloud: "Let me hear in the morning of your merciful love, for in you I put my trust. Teach me the way I should go, for to you I lift up my soul" (Psalm 143:8).

The first hour of Joseph's day is set aside for prayer. Once settled in his morning routine, Joseph centers himself in silence and asks the Lord to guide him in his prayer. The words of Psalm 18 rise from his heart, and Joseph begins to chant: "I love you, O LORD, my strength. The LORD is my rock, and my fortress, and my deliverer, my God, my rock, in whom I take refuge." Joseph's heart moves through Psalm 18 and other psalms, which he knows word for word by memory. The psalms still him into silence, and Joseph spends the rest of his time in focused listening to the Lord.

As the morning unfolds, Joseph's attention soon turns to his carpenter's work. Let us imagine Joseph's hands in careful labor as he asks for inspiration: "Unless the LORD builds the house, those who build it labor in vain" (Psalm 127:1). Throughout the day, he stops to maintain a rhythm of work and prayer. Let us imagine Joseph pausing at noontime and offering the following words to the Lord: "I will give thanks to the LORD with my whole heart; I will tell of all your wonderful deeds. I will be glad and exult in you, I will sing praise to your name, O Most High" (Psalm 9:1-2).

Finally, let us imagine the day's end. Joseph kneels beside his bed and makes a thorough examination of conscience. After a relentlessly honest examination of his heart, Joseph ends the day with the same psalm he began the day as he whispers, "Have mercy on me, O God, according to your merciful love, according to your abundant mercy blot out my transgressions" (Psalm 51:1).

Today's spiritual exercise

Joseph lived in a rhythm of work and prayer. Set the alarms on your phone so that you stop at 9:00 AM, noon, and 3:00 PM. At 9:00 AM, read Psalm 127 and ask the Lord to guide your day. At noon, read Psalm 23. At 3:00 PM, read Psalm 121. Before you go to bed, read Psalm 51. Ask the Lord that you might love the psalms the same way that Joseph loved the psalms.

Day 2
BETROTHED

Matthew 1:18 reminds us that Joseph was a husband, betrothed to Mary. Let us ask the Holy Spirit to help us enter into the ritual of betrothal and the moment when Joseph made his formal and public commitment to the Blessed Mother.

It is a beautiful day in Nazareth, a tiny village in the hills, twelve miles southwest of the Sea of Galilee, composed of approximately two hundred families. A small crowd of relatives and friends has gathered outside Joachim and Anne's home, Mary's parents. Outside the front door is a large square marriage canopy known as a *huppah*, symbolic that a new household is being established.

In the center under the canopy stands Joseph with Mary. Joseph's heart beats to the nervous anticipation within him. His nerves are not out of anxiety or fear. Instead, his heart often accelerates when he sees Mary. He loves her deeply, yet with a sacred reverence that drives him to love Mary on her terms, not his. Mary stands near Joseph with silent, profound gratitude that God has blessed her with a man such as Joseph. She smiles within as she notices Joseph's nervous excitement, for Mary has always felt safe with Joseph's reverence for her.

The local synagogue's rabbi soon quietens the crowd.

After the usual benediction over the wine, he says words similar to these: "Blessed are you O, Lord our God, King of the universe, who has sanctified your people with your commandments. And blessed are you O, Lord our God, King of the universe, who has sanctified your people with the law of marriage." The rabbi, with a joyous smile, then looks to Joseph. Joseph has saved for months to purchase a poor, simple ring, which is part of the ancient Jewish betrothal ritual. He looks deep into Mary's eyes, and as an unexpected watering of tears fills his gaze, he says to Mary: "Be thou betrothed unto me with this ring in accordance with the laws of Moses and Israel."

With those words, Joseph feels suspended as he beholds Mary's eyes. Then, Joseph closes his eyes. As the rabbi recites the ancient marriage contract, Joseph hears only the blur of words. His full attention is in his praying to love Mary as he loves the Lord, "with all your heart, with all your soul, and with all your mind."

The rabbi soon pauses in a respectful cue that Joseph should open his eyes. As tears of joy hug Joseph's beard, the rabbi recites ancient words of benediction over a cup of wine. Joseph and Mary drink from the cup as a sign of their covenant to one another. After the customary concluding benedictions, a spontaneous eruption of applause announced to the heavens that Joseph is now betrothed to Mary.

Today's spiritual exercise

Read Sirach 26:1-4, 13-16. Imagine that, at the end of the day, Joseph walks with Mary to the entrance of her home. Before he returns to his own home, Mary asks Joseph, "What was in your heart when your eyes were closed during the ritual?" Joseph smiles and looks deep into the eyes of Mary and recites the words of Sirach 26:1-4, 13-16. Be *there* in the moment. Be there *with* them. Listen to Joseph share the sacred words of Sirach with his newly betrothed.

_____

_____

_____

_____

_____

_____

_____

_____

_____

_____

Day 3
LISTEN

Matthew 1:18 states, "She was found with child through the Holy Spirit." Nine simple words. However, those words changed the world and altered Joseph's life. Let us ask the Holy Spirit to help us enter into the moments after Joseph learned of Mary's annunciation conceiving the Lord Jesus in her womb.

Joseph is sitting on the peak of a hilltop in Nazareth as he watches the sunset. With his eyes filled with tears, his memory replays the afternoon's incidents as if in slow motion. This day was not what Joseph expected. Earlier that day, Mary had arranged for Joseph to meet her and their rabbi at the synagogue. Quietly, with profound reverence, the rabbi read Isaiah 7:14: "Therefore the Lord himself will give you a sign; the young woman, pregnant and about to bear a son, shall name him Emmanuel." With his eyes drawn into Mary's eyes and Mary's hand leading him to feel her womb, Joseph was aware that Isaiah's prophecy was now fulfilled in his hearing. After walking Mary to her home, Joseph ascended this hill to savor the silence needed to process all that was within him.

The word "obey" comes from the Latin *obedire*, which means "to listen to." Joseph will do whatever it is that the Lord asks of him but needs to hear the voice of the Lord speak to him about something as extraordinary as the Incarnation. As Joseph stares off into the sunset, his heart is saturated with emotion and the thoughts that crowd his mind. He feels overwhelmed, small, and somewhat stunned. He is surprised with the implications of the news and hears the whispers of his unworthiness. He longs to hear God and listen to the voice of truth. To consent to such an awesome calling, Joseph knows that he will find peace, not *despite* the noise of his heart, but *in* the very disturbance that is threatening his peace. Joseph longs to hear God *in* the noise. He is on this hilltop to listen to God *in* the struggle.

As Joseph watches the sunset, he resists the temptation to run from all that is within him. Instead, engaging his will, he stands firm atop the hilltop and begins to pray the words of Psalm 139: "O Lord, you have searched me and known me! You know when I sit down and when I rise up; you discern my thoughts from afar. You search out my path and my lying down, and are acquainted with all my ways. Even before a word is on my tongue, behold, O Lord, you know it altogether."

The words of the psalm calm Joseph's heart. As the sun fades into the horizon, the silence of the moment draws Joseph into prayer. With so much in his heart, Joseph sits in the silence and *listens*.

Today's spiritual exercise

Read Psalm 139:1-16. Imagine that you are sitting next to Joseph as he sits atop the hill at sunset. Listen to Joseph pray the words of Psalm 139 as he begs the Lord for clarity. Sit in the silence with Joseph. Feel all that is in his heart. Feel all that is in your heart as you are with him. Listen deep within your heart as Joseph seeks to listen to the voice of the Lord.

_____

_____

_____

_____

_____

_____

_____

_____

_____

_____

_____

_____

_____

Day 4
SURRENDER

Matthew's Gospel reveals the details of Joseph's heart from the moment Joseph learned of Mary's annunciation through to his own annunciation (see Matthew 1:18-25). Joseph initially "decided to send her away quietly," ending their betrothal. But Scripture tells us then of Joseph's decision to assent to God's plan. Let us ask the Holy Spirit to help us enter into the moment when Joseph surrendered himself to God's plan.

The angel comes to Joseph in a dream, saying, "Do not fear to take Mary your wife, for that which is conceived in her is of the Holy Spirit." The vivid intensity of the dream has brought Joseph the piercing clarity he needs. A few nights before, Joseph stood on the hilltop above Nazareth and asked God to speak. Now the Lord has responded through the message of the angel. Joseph never expected this. The dream thrusts Joseph from sleep, not in fear but in desire. He is drenched in sweat, and his heart is pounding in both awe and excitement. Joseph feels compelled to return to the hilltop to share his heart with the Lord.

Let us imagine Joseph leaving his home in haste while it is still night and returning to the place where he watched the sun set a few evenings before. He ascends the hill, and a quiet symphony of yellow, orange, and red bursts from the horizon as the sun begins to rise.

Recalling the angel and the message in his dream, Joseph once again stands atop the hill, and this time he prays the words of Psalm 66: "Make a joyful noise to God, all the earth; sing the glory of his name; give to him glorious praise! ... All the earth worships you; they sing praises to you, sing praises to your name. Come and see what God has done: he is awesome in his deeds among men" (Psalm 66:1-2, 4-5).

The long-promised, long-awaited Messiah is now in Mary's womb, and the weight of this reality causes Joseph to fall to his knees. Overwhelmed with humility and gratitude, Joseph lifts his head to gaze toward the heavens. He extends his hands in surrender and prays the words of Psalm 118: "O give thanks to the LORD, for he is good; his mercy endures for ever! ... Out of my distress I called on the LORD; the LORD answered me and set me free. ... I thank you that you have answered me and have become my salvation. ... O give thanks to the LORD, for he is good; for his mercy endures for ever!" (Psalm 118:1, 5, 21, 29).

Today's spiritual exercise

Imagine that you are sitting next to Joseph as he surrenders to the Lord atop the hill at sunrise. Listen to Joseph pray the words of Psalms 66 and 118. Feel all that is in his heart. Feel all that is in your heart as you are with him. Listen deep within your heart as Joseph surrenders.

Day 5
EYES

Let us consider the moment when Joseph told Mary of his yes to God's plan. As we enter into this moment in Joseph's life, let us recall the previous conversation he had with Mary. The last time the two of them spoke, he told her he had decided "to send her away quietly." When Mary received this news, she remained steadfast in the Lord's promise to her. Knowing Joseph's goodness and his love for the Lord, Mary waited. Mary was waiting *for* Joseph, but she was waiting *with* the Lord. As she interceded for Joseph, she often spoke the words of Psalm 130: "I wait for the LORD, my soul waits, and in his word I hope" (Psalm 130:5).

Let us ask the Holy Spirit to help us enter into the scene. As the early morning sun wakens the tiny village of Nazareth, Joseph walks from his sunrise hilltop to the home of Joachim, Anne, and Mary. As Joseph nears the door of Mary's house, he recalls the marriage canopy that stood there for their betrothal, in front of that same door. The memories of the betrothal evoke such strong emotion in Joseph that he stops in his tracks. He stands a few feet from Mary's home, lost in memory.

Mary can see Joseph from the window. As she beholds him standing outside her home, she too remembers their betrothal and the moment she looked deep into Joseph's eyes. She has always been able to read Joseph's heart by looking into his eyes. The last time she did so, he told her of his decision to end their betrothal. But as she beholds him today, she immediately notices something different.

Joseph walks to the door, but Mary arrives first and opens it quickly before he can knock. He is caught off guard, more by the look in her eyes than by anything else. Her eyes silence him. All the words that he rehearsed refuse to come forth. It is as if time has stopped, as the two are suspended in a mutual gaze of love, trust, and gratitude.

Mary's eyes gently glance down at her womb. Joseph, captivated by her, follows her glance and falls to his knees. His kneeling reveals to Mary his change of heart, as he pays homage to the King of Kings whom she carries. Now Mary kneels before Joseph, and they hold each other's gaze once again. It is as if time has stopped.

Joseph, whispering, tells Mary the details of his dream and the message of the angel. Soon silence is all that is left. His forehead moves forward and touches hers. Kneeling before each other, holding each other's hands, their foreheads touch in a timeless silence.

Today's spiritual exercise

Read Psalms 130 and 131. Imagine that you are there with Joseph and Mary as they kneel before each other in surrender. Feel all that is in their hearts. Feel all that is in your heart while you are with them.

Day 6
HOUSE

Between the Jewish rite of betrothal and the wedding ceremony, the husband prepared a house for his wife. Let us imagine the house that Joseph prepared for Mary. Let us ask the Holy Spirit to help us enter into the scene.

Imagine entering the house. You notice the thick wooden beams of the doorframe. Carved into the wood are the sacred words of the *Shema*: "Hear, O Israel: The LORD our God is one LORD; and you shall love the LORD your God with all your heart, and with all your soul, and with all your might. ... And you shall write [these words] on the doorposts of your house and on your gates" (Deuteronomy 6:4-5, 9).

As you step inside, you notice that the open space of the house is intentionally designed for hospitality and welcome. Carved into the stone are the words of Abraham: "My lord, if I have found favor in your sight, do not pass by your servant. Let a little water be brought, and wash your feet, and rest yourselves under the tree, while I fetch a morsel of bread, that you may refresh yourselves, and after that you may pass on—since you have come to your servant" (Genesis 18:3-5).

As you move further into the house, recall the tradition mentioned by the early Church Fathers, that Mary had made a biblical vow of consecration, embracing the fullness of perpetual virginity. Let us imagine that

Joseph has also spent months praying for Mary, sharing with the Lord his longing for her to feel safe and secure. Let us imagine that Joseph has often prayed over Mary's bed, recalling these words: "When a woman vows a vow to the LORD, and binds herself by a pledge, while within her father's house, in her youth, and her father hears of her vow and of her pledge by which she has bound herself, and says nothing to her; then all her vows shall stand, and her every pledge by which she has bound herself shall stand. ... And if she is married to a husband, while under her vows or any thoughtless utterance of her lips by which she has bound herself, and her husband hears of it, and says nothing to her on the day that he hears; then her vows shall stand, and her pledges by which she has bound herself shall stand" (Numbers 30:3-4, 7).

Finally, let us imagine the space reserved for Jesus. In response to his annunciation, Joseph has quickly etched into a stone wall the sacred words of Psalm 127: "Behold, sons are a heritage from the LORD, the fruit of the womb a reward" (Psalm 127:3).

Joseph has exercised his skills as a carpenter in building this house, but there is more to the house than mere wood and stone. Joseph has spent months praying here, and the house now contains expressions of all that was deep within him.

Today's spiritual exercise

Read Psalm 127 and imagine how these words describe the house that Joseph built for Mary. Ask the Holy Spirit to help you enter into this house and reveal to you all that was there.

_____

_____

_____

_____

_____

_____

_____

_____

_____

_____

_____

_____

Day 7
HOME

Jewish custom was such that once the betrothal was satisfied, there was an elaborate wedding celebration. After the wedding, the husband would bring his wife into his home to confirm the completion of their marriage bond.

Let us consider the moment when Joseph brought Mary into the house that they would soon make into a home. Let us ask the Holy Spirit to help us enter into the scene. Joseph's smile brims with joy, and in his excitement he strengthens his clasp of Mary's hand as they walk together toward their home. As they arrive at the door, they each kiss the sacred words of the *Shema* that Joseph has etched in the doorframe. Mary smiles, looks at Joseph, and with tears in her eyes she says, "My people will abide in a peaceful habitation..." Joseph adds the remaining words of the verse as he echoes, "... in secure dwellings, and in quiet resting places" (Isaiah 32:18).

As they enter the house together, Mary pauses in silence, taking in all that Joseph has done. She notices the small details that others might overlook, things that reveal how much time Joseph has spent praying in their home. She turns and looks at Joseph and says, "He who dwells in the shelter of the Most High, who abides in the shadow of the Almighty..." and Joseph joins her as their voices in unison finish the words of these verses: "...will say to the LORD, 'My refuge and my fortress; my God, in whom I trust'" (Psalm 91:1-2).

Mary is filled with delight and gratitude for the house Joseph has made for her. Overcome with tears, she looks at Joseph, but before she can say anything, he says to her, "He who finds a wife finds a good thing, and obtains favor from the LORD" (Proverbs 18:22). Mary places her hand on his heart, looks into his eyes, and says to him, "Truly God is good to the upright, to those who are pure in heart" (Psalm 73:1).

After they have explored their home together, they rest in silence. As they have done many times before, they kneel, facing each other, and Joseph leans forward so that his forehead touches Mary's. Kneeling together this way, holding each other's hands, their foreheads press in what has become their favorite posture in prayer. Joseph recites the words of Psalm 118: "O give thanks to the LORD, for he is good; his mercy endures for ever!"

Today's spiritual exercise

Read Psalm 118. Imagine that you are there with Joseph and Mary as they kneel before each other in the joy of their new home. Feel all that is in their hearts. Feel all that is in your heart as you are with them. Listen deep within your heart and imagine hearing Joseph's voice recite the words of Psalm 118.

ADVENT

The events of Mary's annunciation as well as Joseph's annunciation and his surrender to God's plan give us a glimpse of the man Joseph was. The events surrounding the very first Advent reveal even more.

Imagine for a moment what it was like for Joseph during that month before the birth of Jesus. Just as his betrothal challenged him to surrender to life-changing surprises, the events and circumstances of Advent were filled with unexpected challenges. There was the census that no one was expecting. There was the journey to Bethlehem that no one was expecting. Then, after a two-week pilgrimage that strained his finances and provisions, there was nowhere for them to stay in Bethlehem, which no one was expecting.

For many of us, Advent is a busy time of preparation for Christmas. For many of us, December is filled with shopping, Christmas parties, and extravagant dinners. Imagine what Advent was like for Joseph. He was stretched. He was challenged. He tended to Mary's needs and fought to listen to the voice of God in utter dependency.

Welcome to the very first Advent. Let us continue our journey by looking at these weeks through the eyes of Joseph.

Day 8
CENSUS

Luke's Gospel says, "In those days a decree went out from Caesar Augustus that all the world should be enrolled" (Luke 2:1). Just when his wife is getting settled in their home in anticipation of the Savior's birth, Joseph has to tell her that they must travel more than ninety miles south to his ancestral home of Bethlehem.

Let us ask the Holy Spirit to help us enter into the scene. Joseph is quiet. His heart trusts in the Lord, but his mind has natural questions about the journey, about provisions, and about whether they will reach Bethlehem before Mary goes into labor. At times like this, the noise of his questions seems louder than the whisper of God's voice. Therefore, Joseph returns to the hills of Nazareth seeking silence and longing to hear God speak to his questions. In prayer today, however, there is mostly silence. All that he hears are words of the prophet Isaiah: "For my thoughts are not your thoughts, neither are your ways my ways, says the LORD" (Isaiah 55:8). Sensing that more will be revealed later, Joseph is grateful that he has at last heard something.

Joseph walks straight from the hills to their home and finds Mary wrapped in silence. He enters their home, kissing the *Shema* as he comes inside. It is days like today that the words "with all your heart, and with all your soul, and with all your might" remind Joseph that sometimes life requires all you have to give.

Mary's ability to read Joseph's eyes makes it impossible for him to hide his concern. She stands, waiting for him to tell her what is troubling him. Joseph tells her about the census. Surprised by the news, Mary sits, and as she does, her hands move to protect the child she is carrying. Her thoughts, like Joseph's, linger on the unknown. Joseph is comfortable with silence, but today's silence feels like he does not know what to say instead of the familiar peace that is too deep for words.

Reminded of the words from his earlier prayer, Joseph kneels before his wife and whispers the words from Isaiah: "For my thoughts are not your thoughts, neither are your ways my ways, says the LORD." Joseph smiles as he looks deep into Mary's eyes. He places his hand near the child within and, as if referring to her pregnancy, again says to her, "For my thoughts are not your thoughts, neither are your ways my ways, says the LORD." They both smile, and soon their smile turns to a giggle.

However, the laughter is soon replaced with insight. Joseph stands, takes Mary's hand, and gently leads her to stand. Pressing her hand firmly, he reminds them both of other words from Isaiah: "For as the rain and the snow come down from heaven, and do not return there but water the earth ... so shall my word be that goes forth from my mouth; it shall not return to me empty, but it shall accomplish that which I intend, and prosper in the thing for which I sent it. For you shall go out in joy, and be led forth in peace" (Isaiah 55:10-12).

Today's spiritual exercise

Read Isaiah 55. Listen deep within your heart and imagine hearing Joseph's voice recite the words of that passage.

_____

_____

_____

_____

_____

_____

_____

_____

_____

_____

_____

_____

Day 9
REMEMBERS

Let us ask the Holy Spirit to help us enter into the scene as Joseph leads Mary on the pilgrimage to Bethlehem.

As a just man, Joseph is best understood through the words of Psalm 1, "He is like a tree planted by streams of water" (Psalm 1:3), which is to say Joseph drinks from the Scriptures just as a tree's roots drink from a stream. Much of their pilgrimage to Bethlehem is filled with silence, but in the silence Joseph remembers the sacred pilgrimages that are a part of Israel's story.

He remembers the forty-year pilgrimage of his ancestors through the desert on their way to the Promised Land. As Joseph recalls their wandering in the desert, he ponders two things. First, his thoughts drift toward Moses. Joseph thinks about how Moses must have felt leading all his people, as Joseph leads just Mary and the unborn Jesus. Joseph considers Moses' trust in the Lord and asks for the grace to trust as Moses did. Second, Joseph is reminded of God's provision for Israel on that sacred pilgrimage. The more Joseph thinks of God's provision for his people in the desert, the more his heart rests, and his worry is relieved.

As Joseph walks, he wonders if the great King David walked the same steps he is walking now. David was a shepherd long before he was a king, and he would have spent years walking with his flocks. Then, when he became king, David's life was filled with battles and constant moving from place to place. Joseph remembers the story of David bringing the Ark of the Covenant into Jerusalem, and he is struck by the thought that the new Ark of the Covenant is now entrusted to him. He also remembers the promise God made to David: "When your days are fulfilled, and you lie down with your fathers, I will raise up your offspring after you, who shall come forth from your body, and I will establish his kingdom" (2 Samuel 7:12). At that moment, it dawns on Joseph that this is why the pilgrimage to Bethlehem is essential. He thinks, "Of course, the Messiah must come from the city of David: Bethlehem."

As Joseph walks, he remembers all the pilgrimages he has taken to Jerusalem to celebrate the Passover. He remembers how his father led their family in the Passover meal and how now he must lead his own family in the sacred ritual. He remembers the long days walking to Jerusalem and the Passover meal, which is now connected to Israel's anticipation of the Messiah. As he walks in silence, Joseph begins to wonder how the child in Mary's womb will fulfill the Passover expectation.

God's people have been on pilgrimage before at critical moments in their history. Joseph's pilgrimage is filled with silence, and in the silence, he remembers just how sacred pilgrimage is.

Today's spiritual exercise

Read Exodus 15, the song God's people sang as they began their sacred pilgrimage through the desert. Imagine that you are walking with Joseph to Bethlehem, also in sacred pilgrimage through the desert, as he sings these very same words.

_____

_____

_____

_____

_____

_____

_____

_____

_____

_____

_____

_____

_____

Day 10
SELFLESS

The ninety-mile walk from Nazareth to Bethlehem would have taken about ten days. Much would have been required of Joseph during that journey. Let us ask the Holy Spirit to help us enter further into the heart of Joseph and his sacrifices during this pilgrimage.

Let us consider how this pilgrimage requires Joseph to be selfless in considering Mary's needs. Almost nine months' pregnant, Mary has the same needs as other expectant mothers. She is easily tired and needs more frequent stops for rest and relief. Even with all that is on Joseph's mind, he frequently pauses to ask Mary how she is and what she needs. Let us imagine him continually putting his own needs and desires aside so that he can be more attentive to the needs of his wife.

Let us consider how this pilgrimage also requires Joseph to be selfless about food. As the journey continues, their food supply dwindles. But like every child who will soon be born, Jesus requires more of Mary's nutrients. Mary's appetite has grown, and she naturally needs more of their food for the baby. Let us imagine Joseph eyeing their food supply as he stops to prepare dinner at the day's end. As Joseph surveys what he has set aside for tonight's meal and what will be left, he once again chooses to share more of his portion with Mary. He will fast tonight so that there is a little more food for tomorrow.

This pilgrimage also requires Joseph to be selfless about rest. Remember that all of Israel is affected by the census. Jews from all over are on their way to their own ancestral homes. But pilgrims are not the only ones out and about. There are also those looking to take advantage of the pilgrims. Joseph, as the protector of his family, is on the alert all the time. Imagine Joseph trying to sleep at the end of a long day's journey, only to wake at the slightest sound, the slightest indication that danger is afoot.

Much is required of Joseph during these days. But none of Joseph's selfless sacrifices go unnoticed by Mary. She is aware that he is tending to her needs, for she cannot help but notice other pilgrims on the way. Not every husband acts as Joseph does, and Joseph's virtue quietly moves her. She is also aware of his fasting and knows how hungry he must be. And she is aware of his lack of sleep, for she can see the dark circles under his eyes, even though he never complains about being tired.

Let us ask the Holy Spirit to help us "see" the many sacrifices Joseph made during this pilgrimage.

Today's spiritual exercise

Read Psalm 37. Imagine Joseph exhausted from the day, sleeping at Mary's feet. Imagine Mary smiling with inexpressible gratitude as she remembers Psalm 37:4, acknowledging how blessed she is to have a man like Joseph.

Day 11
RESPONSIBLE

Imagine your heart if you were in Joseph's position when he and Mary arrived in Bethlehem and found "there was no place for them in the inn" (Luke 2:7). No place for them in the inn? Imagine arriving in Bethlehem with your wife ready to give birth to the Savior of the world, and as you frantically try to find a safe place, all you hear is no. What would you think? How would you feel?

In the traditional roles as part of God's design, a husband and father's role is to provide for his family. Many men feel the same burden of responsibility today. Let us ask the Holy Spirit to help us appreciate Joseph's astute awareness of who was ultimately responsible.

Consider Joseph's reliance on God as they near the outskirts of Bethlehem. Joseph does not know where his wife will give birth, but he does know that God knows. It was God, not Joseph, who set all this in motion with Mary's annunciation. God, not Joseph, also provided Elizabeth with a child. And it was God who sent the angel to Joseph in a dream (see Matthew 1:20). It was also God who sent them on pilgrimage to Bethlehem to begin with. Throughout this journey, Joseph has been aware of the trap of false responsibility. Joseph's job is to do whatever the Lord asks. It's the Lord's job to do everything else.

Mary, tired from the journey and intensely focused on the child she is carrying, is not concentrating on *where* she will give birth. She is focused on the fact that she *will* give birth. Mary trusts the Lord, and she trusts Joseph. Therefore, let us imagine Joseph looking deep into Mary's eyes as he tells her that the inn has no place for them. Mary's return glance says to him in reply, "I trust you." Joseph smiles, for Mary's trust in him always elicits his best.

Joseph turns toward the mountain caves outside the city and perhaps feels the Lord prompting him to head there. As he walks, Joseph remembers again who is ultimately responsible. He remembers how God assumed responsibility for leading Israel through the desert, and how the Lord provided passage through the Red Sea, manna from heaven, and water from the rock. He remembers how God assumed responsibility for splitting the Jordan River and leading Israel into the Promised Land. He remembers how God assumed responsibility in choosing Israel as his own possession and promised the coming of the Messiah. He remembers that it is God's responsibility to make good on that promise.

There may be no room in the inn, but Joseph understands this to mean that God has other plans. Joseph never confuses "if" with "how." Joseph never confuses obedience with false responsibility. Joseph knows who is ultimately responsible.

Today's spiritual exercise

Read Psalm 121. Imagine that you are in Bethlehem with Joseph as he hears that there is no place for them in the inn. As Joseph turns to the mountain caves outside the city, he begins to pray the words of this psalm. Listen to his voice and hear his confidence. Feel what is in his heart.

CHRISTMAS

The birth of Jesus Christ looked little like the Hallmark Christmas cards. It also looked very different from what most mothers experience today. Historical tradition places the birth of Christ in a cave outside Bethlehem. There was no bed and no midwife or nurse. The setting of the first Christmas was poor and simple.

However, the real Christmas was marvelously profound. Imagine what it was like for Joseph to hold this baby and see the face of God. Imagine his emotion as he placed the newborn child in Mary's arms. Then, just when you think that is it, imagine the added surprises: the shepherds' visit and their account of the angelic host. The encounter with Simeon and Anna eight days after Jesus' birth was also profound, and their words were piercing. And of course there were the Magi, who came more a year or so later, but whose part in the Christmas story cannot be underestimated.

Looking at the Christmas story through Joseph's eyes will help us appreciate his heart and all that he carried in silence and contemplation. With the birth of Christ, Joseph's role continued to focus on Mary and the newborn child.

Let us enter into the story of Christmas through the eyes and the heart of Joseph.

Day 12
FACE

Let us ask the Holy Spirit to help us enter into the scene of the birth of Jesus Christ. In Joseph's search for a place for Mary to give birth, God has provided a simple cave on the outskirts of Bethlehem. Whether the cave was attached to a home or was simply where the animals gathered, imagine this simple cave serving as the chosen place for the birth of God made flesh.

Joseph is kneeling with Mary, who lies on the damp earthen floor. Joseph looks deep into the eyes of his wife. As he clutches her hand, Joseph whispers to her the words of her annunciation, saying, "The Holy Spirit will come upon you, and the power of the Most High will overshadow you; therefore the child to be born will be called holy, the Son of God." Mary smiles and replies, "For with God nothing will be impossible." Mary breathes, closes her eyes, and the cave is wrapped in silence.

Then, in a moment words cannot describe, it is as if time has stopped. Creation itself is leaning forward with anticipation. And now the sacred silence of that holy night is broken by the sound that humankind has longed to hear: the sudden crying of a newborn child. Jesus Christ is born!

As Joseph takes the infant Jesus in his arms, he is the first person to see the face of God. It seems as if time itself has stopped in adoration. In a moment that feels like an eternity, Joseph beholds Jesus. His eyes fill with tears, and joy bursts from his heart. Then, instinctively, his strong hands gently place the newborn Savior in Mary's arms, and Joseph kneels beside them in humble adoration. Mary kisses the forehead of her baby boy. As she studies the face of her newborn son, Joseph remembers the words of the ancient blessing of God's people: "Thus you shall bless the sons of Israel: you shall say to them, the Lord bless you and keep you: the Lord make his face to shine upon you, and be gracious to you: the Lord lift up his countenance upon you, and give you peace. So shall they put my name upon the people of Israel, and I will bless them" (Numbers 6:23-27).

Joseph speaks the sacred words over the baby and receives them back as a blessing on Mary and himself: "The LORD make his *face* to shine upon you." There, a mere few inches from his own face is the *face of God*. God is not invisible. Joseph is now face to face with God himself.

Today's spiritual exercise

Read Numbers 6:22-27. Imagine that *you* are there with Joseph as Jesus is born. Imagine that *you* are there with Joseph looking at the face of God. Imagine being with Joseph as he kneels in adoration of Jesus while the baby rests in his mother's arms. Be there *with* them. Be there in the scene.

Day 13
DEPEND

Joseph is sitting with his back against the wall of the cave. His feet are warmed by a small fire that he has built for his family. Hours after the birth of Christ, the fatigue of the journey and the birth has caught up with Mary. She is tired and needs rest.

As she holds her baby in her arms, Mary leans against Joseph's chest. She has always felt safe with Joseph, and tonight she appreciates him anew. The glow of the small fire dances with the beauty of Mary's voice as she hums a song to her sleeping son. Overwhelmed with joy, Joseph is taking in all that is this moment.

Soon Mary's voice is silent as fatigue calls her to sleep. She turns her head and, with a simple glance, she asks Joseph to hold Jesus. The strong, rugged hands of the carpenter embrace the baby, and Mary drifts into sleep.

It is quiet, so very, very quiet. In the sacred silence, the words of the angel return to Joseph's heart: "She will bear a son, and you shall call his name Jesus, for he will save his people from their sins." As Joseph savors these words, it dawns on him anew. *This* child, *this* baby, will save people from their sins. The salvation of every human being is dependent on *this* child.

As Joseph watches Jesus sleep, he is astonished that God has chosen to make himself so vulnerable. A newborn child cannot raise himself; he is dependent on his parents. He realizes that *this* child is not merely dependent, but dependent on *him*.

Let us ask the Holy Spirit to help us "feel" all that is in Joseph's heart as he begins to understand how dependent the child is on him. At this moment, Joseph is overwhelmed with awe. Of all the men ever born, God chose one—only one—to be the husband of the mother of God. Of all men, God chose one—only one— to reveal true fatherhood to the Son of God. God chose Joseph to protect and raise the child Jesus. God the Father is depending on Joseph.

As Joseph tenderly holds Jesus, the weight of this moment draws Joseph into prayer. Jesus is dependent on Joseph, and the only way Joseph will be able to fulfill this awesome task is if he himself remains dependent on the Father. Joseph knows he cannot do this on his own. He closes his eyes and asks for help. Then, in the silence, he hears in his heart the words of Isaiah, "For I, the LORD your God, hold your right hand; it is I who say to you, 'Fear not, I will help you'" (Isaiah 41:13).

Today's spiritual exercise

Read Isaiah 41. Imagine that *you* are there with Joseph as he receives Jesus from Mary's arms. Imagine that *you* are there with Joseph as he holds Jesus. Be there *with* them. Be there in the scene. Listen to Joseph's breathing as he holds the infant Jesus. Feel what is in Joseph's heart as he holds the Christ child.

Day 14
SHEPHERDS

Ancient tradition places the birth of Christ in a cave outside Bethlehem. Luke tells us that "in that region there were shepherds out in the field, keeping watch over their flock by night" (Luke 2:8). The shepherds were familiar with the mountain caves for, as Pope Benedict tells us, the "rocky caves had been used as stables since ancient times."[1]

After walking with their flock during the day, shepherds would herd their sheep together by nightfall. Then the shepherds would take turns keeping watch, protecting the sheep from predators through the night.

Let us ask the Holy Spirit to help us enter into the scene of the shepherd's visit. Joseph is sitting with his back against the cave wall. Mary has just placed Jesus in the manger and is sitting with Joseph, leaning on his chest. The reality of all that has happened is still sinking in when, suddenly, there is noise and commotion outside the cave. Joseph gets up and moves quickly to the entrance. Mary, with a similar protective instinct, instantly moves to the manger. Joseph's heart pounds and his fists clench as he sees the faces of several men outside. But he also notices their contagious joy, and cautiously he stands aside to let them look inside. Instantly they kneel in homage. Surprised by their reverence, Joseph glances toward Mary and then back at the strangers.

The oldest shepherd begins to tell Joseph what happened to them, and the other shepherds chime in. They were keeping watch over the sheep, and a sudden light lit up the night sky, and an angel said the Messiah had been born and they would find him here. And then hundreds of angels appeared singing, filling the sky with glory!

Still cautious and protective, Joseph nods in wonder and steps aside to join his wife, letting the men come into the cave. They kneel by the manger now in homage and adoration, and the excitement and noise are soon stilled in deep silence and awe.

Today's spiritual exercise

Read Luke 2:8-19. Imagine that *you* are there with the shepherds. Imagine that *you* are the shepherd who is keeping the night watch when the angels appear. Be there in the scene. Imagine seeing the sudden light and waking the others. Imagine hearing the angels' message and listening to their glorious singing. Then imagine running with the others to the cave where Jesus lies in the manger. And now you are kneeling in that sacred place, with the baby just a few inches away and Joseph and Mary kneeling beside you.

Day 15
PRESENTATION

The story of the Nativity shifts from the intimacy of the cave to Jerusalem and the Temple. Scripture tells us that "when the time came for their purification according to the law of Moses, they brought him up to Jerusalem to present him to the Lord." It also mentions that Simeon and Anna were in the Temple at that time (see Luke 2:22-38).

Let us ask the Holy Spirit to help us enter into the scene. Joseph is familiar with the Temple in Jerusalem. He makes a pilgrimage to the Temple three times every year for the feasts of Passover, Pentecost, and Tabernacles. As Joseph walks toward Jerusalem with Mary and the infant Jesus, his thoughts linger on memories of his childhood, when he made similar pilgrimages with his own father. As they near Jerusalem, the familiar sight of the Temple's sprawling grandeur and the thick fragrance of incense and burnt offerings stir Joseph's soul. The ordinary bustle of pilgrims mingles with the chants of priests praying the psalms. The psalms have always elicited emotion in Joseph. As he ascends the steps with his wife and the Christ child, he begins to sing quietly the opening words of Psalm 122: "I was glad when they said to me, 'Let us go to the house of the LORD!'"

As Joseph, Mary, and Jesus enter the Temple, they are asked their son's name, and Joseph recalls the sacred words of the angel as he says, "His name is Jesus." With that, Joseph glances toward Mary, and she whispers to Joseph in reply, "For he will save his people from their sins" (Matthew 1:21).

Soon after, Joseph and Mary offer the customary sacrifice according to Jewish law, "a pair of turtledoves, or two young pigeons." Joseph is familiar with the sacrifice rites of the Temple; however, today's offering strikes a chord in his heart. The blood from the birds is poured out on the same altar where, later in the year, the priests will pour out the blood of the Passover lambs. Joseph begins to ponder what might be asked of Jesus to fulfill the meaning of his name and to "save his people from their sins."

The events of this day unfold with remarkable inexpectancies. Simeon's prayer and blessing over Joseph and Mary penetrate Joseph's heart. Anna's thanksgiving adds to the extraordinary feel of the day. First it was the visit of the shepherds. Today it is the unexpected encounters with Simeon and Anna. Joseph is beginning to sense that the birth of Jesus will have different effects on his life than perhaps he expected. Furthermore, there are Simeon's troubling words to Mary: "A sword will pierce through your own soul also." The thought of Mary's heart being pierced alarms the protector in Joseph, and he ponders what these words can mean.

As the events of Jesus' presentation conclude, Joseph finds himself alone with Mary and the infant Jesus. The

Holy Family is wrapped in silence as the parents marvel at all that has been said about the child.

Today's spiritual exercise

Read Luke 2:22-38. Imagine that you are there with Joseph and Mary. Enter into the scene and listen to what is said. Specifically, so that you may further experience what was in Joseph's heart, sit with Joseph and Mary as they take in the events of the day. Ask Joseph to reveal to you what he experienced.

Day 16
MAGI

After their time in Jerusalem, Joseph, Mary, and Jesus returned to Bethlehem. We know this because of the account of in Matthew 2 and the story of the Magi. Before we ask the Holy Spirit to help us enter the scene, let us appreciate who is in it. Magi were members of the Persian priestly caste. Pope Benedict XVI writes that they were "custodians of religious and philosophical knowledge that had developed in that area and continued to be cultivated there." He also notes that "the wise men from the east are a new beginning. They represent the journeying of humanity toward Christ. ... Not only do they represent the people who have found the way to Christ: they represent the inner aspiration of the human spirit," the yearning of all humanity.[2]

At the time of the Magi's visit, Jesus was no longer a newborn. He was most likely just under two years old, and by then, Mary and Jesus were staying in someone's home. With that background, let us ask the Holy Spirit to help us imagine the unexpected visit of these mysterious men from the East.

It is evening. The splendid radiance of this evening's sunset has faded, and the blanket of night is revealing the full array of stars. The night sky has been especially beautiful of late, and many people have noticed the appearance of an extraordinary star. Tonight Joseph and Mary are standing outside, and Jesus is sitting on Joseph's shoulders. Joseph's right hand holds the toddler steady while with his left he holds Mary's hand. The two parents drink in the evening's beauty. Mary has just commented on the radiance of the unique star, and Joseph responds with the words of a psalm: "The heavens are telling the glory of God; and the firmament proclaims his handiwork" (Psalm 19:1). They both smile and return to the house.

Soon after they settle inside, there is a knock on the door. Joseph strides to the door as the toddler Jesus follows him, just as little boys often follow their daddy. Joseph opens the door, and Jesus pokes his head from behind Joseph's legs. Before Joseph can invite the visitors in, three exotic, strangely dressed men catch sight of Jesus and fall to their knees. Joseph is stunned, but Jesus merely watches them. These travelers from the East pay homage to the two-year-old Jesus while Joseph and Mary take in the scene.

The men tell Joseph and Mary who they are and where they have come from. One of them comments that we are all searching for something. Joseph smiles and responds, "We are searching for *someone*." Certainly, whether we know it or not, deep within us all is what Pope Benedict calls "the inner aspiration of the human spirit."[3] We are all looking. We are all searching.

As their conversation with Joseph and Mary continues, the Magi hand them their treasures, gifts of gold, frankincense, and myrrh. They tell their stories—of following the star and of all that was within them when they saw the Christ child. Joseph and Mary remain in awe, silently receiving the profound experience of this extraordinary visit.

Today's spiritual exercise

Read Matthew 2:1-12. Imagine that you are there with Joseph and the Magi. Specifically, so that you may further experience what was in Joseph's heart, enter into the scene and listen to what is said. Be with them *in* the scene. Ask Joseph to reveal to you what he experienced.

_____

_____

_____

_____

_____

_____

_____

_____

_____

_____

_____

EGYPT

The visit of the Magi was a joyous encounter. Imagine what it was like to meet men who had traveled hundreds of miles with the sole purpose of giving homage to the Son of God and Son of Mary. Their visit would have been filled with stories of foreign lands and of their study of the star that led them. Their gifts of gold, frankincense, and myrrh would have provided a new lens to see the reality of Christ's identity and his mission to save the whole world.

However, all that joy would have been arrested by the mention of Herod and his interest in the child. Imagine what was in Joseph's heart when he realized that Herod was hunting not just any child but *this* child.

The dream that later woke Joseph and propelled him into the flight to Egypt required much from him. He had to protect his family from thieves and robbers. He had to find his way to Egypt with no map or previous knowledge of the route. From a man of whom so much was asked, more would be asked.

The flight to Egypt and the Holy Family's years there would have confirmed Joseph in his role as protector and provider. This season in their lives is hidden and often overlooked. Let us listen to Joseph's heart now as we go with him to Egypt.

Day 17
DREAM

Let us ask the Holy Spirit to help us imagine how the evening of the Magi's visit ends with extraordinary grace. The strange visitors from the East join Mary and Joseph for a meal. At the end of the meal, Joseph hoists Jesus up on his shoulders, and everyone goes outside. The Magi have already explained what they know about "the star." Joseph feels a keen sense of peace, and his thoughts drift to the visit of the shepherds on the night Jesus was born. With joy in his heart, Joseph asks his visitors to tell them more about their travels through the land of Israel.

But Joseph's inner peace is shattered when the Magi describe their visit with Herod. The story does not sit well with Joseph, especially when the Magi mention how important it was to Herod to know exactly where they would find the long-prophesied King of the Jews. After bidding farewell to the Magi, Joseph sends Mary and Jesus inside and spends a few moments alone outside. His spirit has been disturbed by the mention of Herod, and he asks the Father for help in understanding his intuitive unrest. Joseph's prayer leaves him trusting God, and he goes back inside to help Mary with their evening routine with Jesus.

At Jesus' bedtime, Joseph blesses the child and then talks quietly and comfortably with his wife. Mary and

Joseph wind the day down together. His last words to her are usually those of Scripture: "He who finds a wife finds a good thing, and obtains favor from the LORD" (Proverbs 18:22). With those words, Mary falls asleep, leaving Joseph to one of his favorite moments of the day, when he can look at Mary in gratitude and purity.

When Joseph falls sleeps, however, the night changes direction. Matthew tells us that "an angel of the Lord appeared to Joseph in a dream and said, 'Rise, take the child and his mother, and flee to Egypt, and remain there till I tell you; for Herod is about to search for the child, to destroy him'" (Matthew 2:13). As with his dream before Jesus' birth, Joseph is thrust from sleep. He is drenched in sweat, and his heart is pounding. There is an urgency in the air, and Joseph can feel it.

The words "Rise, take the child and his mother, and flee to Egypt, and remain there till I tell you" are seared in his mind. And the words "Herod is about to search for the child, to destroy him" have pierced his heart. How can he protect this child against such a powerful man? Joseph watches Mary sleep and collects his thoughts so as not to alarm her. Squeezing her hand gently but firmly, he wakes her. He does not need to say much, for Mary can read Joseph's eyes, and they express the urgency of the moment. Within minutes Mary and Joseph have collected their belongings and are ready for their journey.

As Mary holds Jesus in her arms, Joseph stands outside the house, looks to the sky, and takes his first steps toward Egypt.

Today's spiritual exercise

Read Matthew 2:13-15. Imagine that you are there with Joseph as he wakes. Enter into the scene and feel what is in Joseph's heart. Feel the urgency of the moment.

_____

_____

_____

_____

_____

_____

_____

_____

_____

_____

_____

_____

_____

_____

Day 18
HUNTED

The Holy Family must flee Bethlehem. Let us ask the Holy Spirit to help us enter into the scene. It is midnight, and an ominous blanket of evil cloaks the night. Joseph was awakened by the message of an angel, who said, "Take the child and his mother, and flee to Egypt ... for Herod is about to search for the child, to destroy him." Joseph, Mary, and Jesus are now hurrying to escape. Joseph does not know how to get to Egypt, but what he does know is that Herod is hunting.

The dark of night has provided a covering for the Holy Family, hiding them from Herod's soldiers. Joseph wants to get to the foothills of Bethlehem, where it will be easier for him and Mary to travel in safety. But with each twist and turn of their descent down the mountain, another band of Herod's horsemen comes charging up past them. Now, just as another troop passes, Joseph's foot slips, setting rocks tumbling. In a moment of gripping fear for Joseph and Mary, the horses stop and the soldiers reverse their tracks. Herod's soldiers heard the rocks fall and suspect that someone from Bethlehem is afoot.

Joseph's heart is pounding as the horsemen ride toward them. The Holy Family quickly slips between two boulders. The crevice provides just enough space to hide, and in the dark of the night they cannot be seen.

Terrified, Joseph can see soldiers dismount to look for them. He can hear the snorting of horses mere yards away. He can hear demonic taunting as Herod's soldiers mock "the king of the Jews."

The horrific sounds of murder now reach them from atop the mountain, from within the city of Bethlehem. Matthew tells us of the evil of that night. As every child in Bethlehem is killed, Joseph and Mary can hear the heartrending cries of their mothers' wailing. Joseph's hand covers Mary's mouth so that her sobs will not be heard, and his fingers are soon wet with her tears.

After what feels like an eternity, Herod's soldiers give up their hunt. They mount their horses and charge up the mountain to carry out Herod's hate-filled orders. Joseph and Mary stay frozen in their hiding space until it is clear the path is safe.

Joseph rises and clutches the hands of his wife and the toddler. As they continue their descent, the wailing of distraught mothers grows fainter. Joseph knows that they will not return to Bethlehem soon. All that lies before him is the unknown of Egypt. But that is how the journey to Bethlehem started two years ago. God provided for them in Bethlehem, and Joseph is certain that the Lord will provide for them in Egypt, too.

Today's spiritual exercise

Read Matthew 2:16-18. Imagine that you are there with Joseph as he leads Mary and Jesus out of Bethlehem. Enter into the scene and feel what is in Joseph's heart. Feel the urgency of the moment. Be with the Holy Family as they flee.

Day 19
"I"

Bethlehem is only five miles from Jerusalem. We do not know whether Joseph had ever been to Bethlehem prior to the census, but we do know that Joseph had been to Jerusalem. Under Mosaic Law, all adult male Jews were required to make a pilgrimage to Jerusalem three times every year for the feasts of Passover, Pentecost, and Tabernacles. So even if Joseph had never been to Bethlehem, he knew how to get to Jerusalem, and Bethlehem was only five miles away.

Egypt was not five miles away; it was five-hundred miles away. It is unlikely that Joseph had ever been to Egypt, and it is unlikely that he knew how to get there. Let us consider, then, what the angel was asking of him when the angel said, "Rise, take the child and his mother, and flee to Egypt, and remain there till I tell you" (Luke 2:13).

Let us consider the details of the angel's message so we can appreciate Joseph's feelings as the journey begins. Imagine being awakened during the night by the message of an angel. Imagine being told you have to flee *now*. Imagine being told that Herod is seeking to destroy Jesus. Joseph must act quickly, and he and Mary and the child are gone almost before they are fully awake. Joseph does not know where Egypt is or how to get there. For the moment he knows only that they must get down the mountain. But even that brief journey is terrifying amid the chaos of murderous Roman soldiers and parents who are wild with grief. What must it have been like to leave Bethlehem during the murder of the Holy Innocents?

"Rise, take the child and his mother, and flee to Egypt, and remain there till I tell you." These words have given rise to strong feelings in Joseph. But the most powerful word he hears in the message of the angel is the smallest one: *I*. "Remain there till *I* tell you." God is promising Joseph that he will speak to him, and Joseph trusts this promise because he has heard the voice of the Lord before. Joseph knows the voice of the *I*.

Let us ask the Holy Spirit to help us walk with Joseph as the Holy Family travels to Egypt. The five-hundred-mile pilgrimage will take about a month and a half. Much of each day is spent in silence, and both Mary and Joseph remain attuned to the voice of God throughout the day. Joseph is listening to the voice of the Lord as it instructs him not only where to go but also where not to go, when to speak to others and when to stay silent to avoid danger and remain in safety. With all the unknowns that are a part of this journey, Joseph is clinging to the voice of the Lord.

Today's spiritual exercise

Read Jeremiah 29:11-14. Imagine that you are with Joseph as he walks to Egypt. Enter into the scene and ask God to help you feel just how quiet Joseph's heart was. Listen to the silence and ask Joseph to teach you about the voice of the Lord.

Day 20
SCRATCH

Let us ask the Holy Spirit to help us appreciate everything that was asked of Joseph in the experience of Egypt. Once the Holy Family arrives in Egypt, Joseph has to start from scratch. In the first century, there were significant settlements of Jews in Egypt. So the Holy Family's transition into Egypt may have been eased by the familiar presence of other Jews who lived there.

As the provider for his family, Joseph needs work. The transition to a new land and a new community certainly would make it more challenging to earn a living. Living in Egypt would have required much of Joseph and the Holy Family. Starting from scratch requires everything.

Let us ask the Holy Spirit to help us appreciate what life in Egypt would have looked like during their first days there. Mountains flank the eastern border of Egypt, which rests on the western edge of the Red Sea. This mountain range may well have been on their walking path from Bethlehem to Egypt. Let us imagine that Joseph found an empty cave in the mountainside. The Holy Family has settled into this cave and made it their own.

As a skilled carpenter and laborer, Joseph builds furniture and makes other improvements to help Mary and Jesus feel safer and more at home. He also makes useful things to sell. The rocky terrain provides very little by way of sustenance, so Joseph walks to the neighboring town every day to sell what he has made. Although he is new to the area, people appreciate his patience in trying to communicate and his peaceful spirit. He is becoming well known in the small town for his craftsmanship.

Joseph trusts in the Lord, but he naturally wonders about the basics of survival for his family. When he is away at the market, his thoughts are often with Mary and Jesus. He worries about their safety and about what they may need during the day.

Starting from scratch means having no reserves, none of the resources that people build up over time and rely on when things get complicated. The lack of anything extra requires Joseph to live in the present moment. Every day he is forced to depend on the Lord for provision.

Starting from scratch also means that there are no family or friends nearby. And the language barrier makes it difficult for Joseph to make new friends or find confidants.

Today's spiritual exercise

Read Exodus 14, especially verse 14. Imagine having to start over from scratch in a land where you neither speak the language nor have anyone to help you. Now enter into the scene as the Holy Family starts over in Egypt. Be with them. Be with Joseph. Ask the Holy Spirit to show you what it really means to start from scratch.

Day 21
LEADER

Joseph did not know how long they would be in Egypt, but he did know this: Living Jewish in Egypt would require him to be his family's spiritual leader.

Let us consider Joseph as the spiritual leader of his family, especially while they are in Egypt. Joseph returns from the market and arrives at his home in the late afternoon. As always, Mary is delighted to see him. And as always, Jesus sprints toward Joseph at the first sight of him. With his strong hands, strengthened by years of carpentry work, Joseph lifts Jesus high above his head and twirls him in a circle. He tosses Jesus in the air and catches him, laughing. Few things make Joseph smile the way Jesus' laughter does.

Jesus is now four years old. Every night, Joseph kneels with Jesus before sleep. On this Friday night, as the Sabbath begins, the child Jesus asks Joseph why he likes to walk on the mountainside. Joseph responds, "So that I can hear the voice of the Lord." Jesus smiles, and as he does so Joseph is overwhelmed again to think that he, Joseph, has been chosen to model for Jesus how to listen attentively to the Lord.

At the young age of four, Jesus already has a few favorite psalms. Joseph asks Jesus which psalm they should sing tonight. Jesus playfully closes his eyes for a quick moment, and then as he opens them, he says with the

voice of an innocent child, "The LORD is my shepherd."
Quickly Joseph joins him: "I shall not want; he makes
me lie down in green pastures" (Psalm 23:1). The prayer
deepens as Mary joins in. As she enters the room, she
kneels next to Joseph, takes his hand, and the three of
them pray the rest of the psalm together.

The next day is Saturday, the Sabbath day. Here in
Egypt, Joseph has established a weekly routine for the
Sabbath. He teaches Jesus about the history of Israel,
especially their history in Egypt. Today, he is teaching
Jesus the story of the Passover and the Exodus, how the
Lord brought their people out of Egypt and into their
homeland. Jesus interrupts Joseph's story and asks, "Are
we going to leave Egypt and go back to our home?"

Joseph smiles. He looks at Mary and she smiles. Both
of them long to return home. Joseph responds to Jesus
as he always does, saying that they will do whatever the
Lord tells them to do.

Today's spiritual exercise

Read Psalm 23. Imagine that *you* are kneeling next to
Joseph as he and Jesus sing the psalms at night. Listen
to the strong voice of Joseph. Listen for the tender voice
of Jesus and the purity of a four-year-old singing with
his dad. Be *with* them. Be *in* the scene.

NAZARETH

Most of Jesus' life, and the remainder of Joseph's life, would take place in Nazareth. Let us together imagine ancient Nazareth. It was a small town and a poor one, and life there would have been simple and quiet. Most likely the community was tight knit. We can imagine the rejoicing of their parents and family and friends when Joseph, Mary, and Jesus arrived back home.

So much would happen in that home in Nazareth. Jesus would learn how to learn. Joseph would teach him the Scriptures, especially the psalms. He would teach him to pray and to listen in prayer. It is in Nazareth that Jesus would come to know, in his sacred humanity, the fullness of the Father's voice and, in it, the fullness of his identity.

So much would happen in Nazareth. Joseph would be a dad to Jesus and Jesus would live as his son. Jesus would work with Joseph, play with Joseph, and laugh with Joseph.

Jesus would witness the way that Joseph loved Mary as his wife, how he cared for her and honored her. Jesus would see firsthand how Joseph protected Mary's purity, thus modeling for Jesus what a real man, a husband, and a father look like.

So much would happen in Nazareth, and it is there that our journey takes us.

Day 22
HOME

When the angel told Joseph to flee Bethlehem with Mary and the child, he also told Joseph to remain in Egypt "till I tell you." This is what Joseph did. Matthew tells us that "when Herod died, behold, an angel of the Lord appeared in a dream to Joseph in Egypt, saying, 'Rise, take the child and his mother, and go to the land of Israel, for those who sought the child's life are dead'" (Matthew 2:19-20). So Joseph led Mary and Jesus out of Egypt and settled the Holy Family in Nazareth.

Ancient Nazareth had a population of less than five hundred. But it was just three or four miles from Sepphoris, a quickly growing city of nearly twenty-five thousand. Many of the laborers who worked in Sepphoris lived in Nazareth, which was close enough for commerce but far enough away to have a different atmosphere. Nazareth was small and quaint, with lots of silence and solitude. Nazareth was quiet.

The atmosphere of Nazareth would have influenced the atmosphere of Joseph and Mary's home. It had been many years since Joseph built this home for Mary during their betrothal. Those few months after she moved in, before they left for the census in Bethlehem, had been some of the happiest of Joseph's life. Now, after their time in Egypt, their return to this particular home is a great blessing for them.

Let us ask the Holy Spirit to bring us into the home of the Holy Family in Nazareth. Three words perhaps characterize their home: silence, presence, and hospitality. Let us first imagine how silence would have been a part of life in Nazareth. Remember that there are no televisions, screens, or technology. The simplicity of life outside the home complements the silence within. Joseph is very comfortable with silence and comfortable giving Mary her own "space" for silence. It would have been intentional for him to foster a spirit of contemplation in the home, an atmosphere conducive to Jesus' human maturation.

The silence of their home fosters attention to the present moment and their presence to one another in all they do. Mary is confident that she is seen and heard. Jesus understands that he is known and loved.

Considering ancient Jewish culture and the ordered human nature of Joseph, Mary, and Jesus, the home in Nazareth surely overflows with hospitality. Let us imagine just how safe visitors feel in Joseph's home. The Holy Family never fail to provide an authentic welcome, sincere interest, good conversation, and honest concern.

Today's spiritual exercise

Read Proverbs 3:33, 15:6, and 24:3-4. Imagine what an entire day would have felt like in the home of the Holy Family. Imagine yourself there as a guest in their home. Imagine yourself spending the morning in silence and prayer just as they often did. Imagine the joy and laughter of the conversation that flowed so easily in their home. Imagine the quality of hospitality as they shared meals and daily life with visitors, and evenings with deeper conversation. Imagine Joseph as he prayed over Jesus and Mary before they went to sleep. Be *there*. Imagine *yourself* in their home.

Day 23
PURITY

I have often seen paintings that depict Joseph as an older man. Some people assume that he was much older than Mary because he died before Jesus began his public ministry. Some believe that God wed Mary to an older husband who, because of his age, would not experience sexual temptation the way a younger man would.

I am in complete harmony and agreement with the Church's teaching that Mary died a virgin and lived her life in a perpetual state of purity. In my opinion, however, to say that this happened because Joseph was older and did not face temptation does not honor Joseph. I don't think Mary lived in perpetual purity because Joseph was never tempted. I think she lived in such purity because Joseph was a well integrated and holy man. God blessed Mary with marriage to a man of holiness, not a man who could not contain himself until he was old.

Let us ask the Holy Spirit to help us appreciate Joseph's holiness and his reverence for Mary's purity. Let us imagine the purity in which Joseph sees Mary. Joseph does not lust after Mary. She is most likely beautiful. But Joseph is an integrated man who has the capacity for self-mastery. Mary feels safe and seen by Joseph, and she forever trusts how he looks at her.

Let us imagine the way that Joseph expresses his affection for her. Joseph's love for Mary is not functional but personal. There is never a violation of boundaries, for Joseph's heart is ordered toward God's design. This means that Joseph has great affection for Mary and feels all that a husband feels when he loves his wife.

Let us imagine too how safe Mary feels with Joseph. Because Mary feels seen and secure, she feels free to be who she is, who God created her to be. She trusts Joseph's self-awareness, self-mastery, and self-possession and therefore never questions his self-gift, how he looks at her or how he feels for her.

Let us consider that God chose one man in all of history to do what Joseph did. He chose one man in all of history to live in a perfectly full and perfectly chaste marriage with Mary. God chose this man to model for Jesus how men can perfectly integrate their sexuality. He chose one man to live this, and that man was Joseph.

Today's spiritual exercise

Read Psalm 119:1-16. Imagine that it is late in the evening. Joseph is sleeping and Mary is praying before she retires. *You* are there. You are there *with* Mary. You are there with her in the home of the Holy Family. Listen to Mary recite the words of these verses as she looks at Joseph. Listen to Mary use these exact words to describe the man God has provided for her as husband.

Day 24
DAD

The *Catechism of the Catholic Church* teaches that "the language of faith ... draws on the human experience of parents, who are in a way the first representatives of God for man" (CCC 239). One of the roles of a dad is to live his life in such a way that, through him, his children experience elements of God the Father. The way they experience such things as love, mercy, forgiveness, and encouragement all point to those very same attributes in God the Father. Let us consider today the fact that God the Father chose Joseph, the one man in all of history who best exemplified the Father's attributes, so that Jesus could learn about God the Father through him.

Let us ask the Holy Spirit to help us appreciate some of the ways God the Father revealed himself to Jesus through Joseph. Joseph knows well the power of example, for he is inspired by his own father's life and witness. Knowing well a dad's responsibility to set the standard for his son, Joseph first teaches Jesus how to pray by the way he prays. Let us imagine Joseph rising early every morning so that he can offer the best moments of the day to the Lord.

On one particular morning, Joseph is awake early as he usually is, praying the psalms. Jesus also wakes early this morning. Just as most little boys instinctively want to spend time with their dad, Jesus loves spending time with

Joseph. Seeing that Joseph is praying, Jesus wants to pray, too, because he wants to be like his dad. Imagine Jesus kneeling right beside Joseph. Joseph intentionally keeps his eyes closed and continues praying. Jesus mirrors what Joseph is doing as he also closes his eyes and begins to pray the psalms that Joseph has taught him.

Joseph has also taught Jesus about the dignity of work and the importance of offering everything to the Lord. Later that day, Joseph asks Jesus to help him with a carpentry project. With great excitement, Jesus runs outside to assist Joseph. However, Jesus knows from previous experience that there is something that Joseph will do before they begin their work. Joseph extends his hands and says words like these: "Blessed are you, Lord our God, King of the universe, who has sanctified work and made it holy. Bless our hands and our minds and all our work today so that we may glorify you in all we do."

Today, as they are working together, two Roman soldiers pass by and casually mock Joseph and insult him. Joseph remains calm and courteous. In Joseph's example of virtue, prudence, and command of himself, Jesus is learning the value of mercy, humility, and charity.

Joseph may not have been the biological father of Jesus, but Joseph fulfilled the role of a dad. And as Joseph did so, God the Father revealed himself through Joseph to Jesus.

Today's spiritual exercise

Read Psalm 37:1-7. In your imaginative prayer, spend the day with Jesus as he spends the day with Joseph. Ask the Holy Spirit to show you how Joseph fulfills the role of a dad for Jesus.

_____

_____

_____

_____

_____

_____

_____

_____

_____

_____

_____

_____

_____

Day 25
LOST

Under Mosaic Law, all Jews were required to make an annual pilgrimage to Jerusalem for the feast of Passover. Luke tells us the story of Joseph and Mary finding Jesus in the Temple after Passover one year (see Luke 2:41-50). Let us ask the Holy Spirit to draw us into the moment in Joseph's life when Jesus was found.

Passover is one of Joseph's favorite times of the year, and this particular spring has been extraordinarily beautiful. The pilgrimage from Nazareth, more than ninety miles, took five days, and Joseph savored this year's conversation with Jesus. Now twelve years old, Jesus is coming into his own, and his understanding of God and the Scriptures is unusual, far beyond what Joseph would expect of a boy his age.

At the end of their time in Jerusalem, Joseph and Mary join their extended family to travel back to Nazareth in a caravan. This year Jesus has been much more articulate and intentional in conversation about the Scriptures, and they assume he is talking with others in the family group. At the end of a full day's journey, Joseph asks Mary if she had seen Jesus. When Mary shakes her head, Joseph begins to worry. They ask family members, but no one has seen the twelve-year-old child. Joseph and Mary realize that he is not with them. Their only option is to return to the massive crowds packing Jerusalem and look for him there.

Passover crowds can be overwhelming, and even though many of the pilgrims have begun to return to their homes, there are still over a half million people packing the streets of Jerusalem. Mary and Jesus spend three days frantically looking for their son. Exhausted and anxious, Joseph finally suggests that they go to the Temple. At this time of year, the Temple is the most crowded place in all of Jerusalem.

There at last they find the boy "sitting among the teachers, listening to them and asking them questions; and all who heard him were amazed at his understanding and his answers" (Luke 2:47). Joseph is astonished, but he also knows how the anxiety for Jesus has affected Mary. Out of consideration for her, Joseph excuses himself and gently leads Jesus away from the group to his mother. Joseph is surprised by Jesus' response: "How is it that you sought me? Did you not know that I must be in my Father's house?"

Eventually, as the Holy Family squeezes through the enormous crowds to make their way out of Jerusalem, Joseph continues to ponder Jesus' question in the Temple. Joseph places this incident beside the rest of his experience of Jesus this Passover and smiles in appreciation of what he senses is unfolding.

Today's spiritual exercise

Read Luke 2:41-50. In your prayer, imagine all that is in the Scripture passage. Be *with* Joseph, by his side, as he finds Jesus in the Temple.

Day 26
OBEDIENCE

Joseph knows who Jesus is and, ultimately, *whose* Jesus is. Thus, Joseph is aware that he has a very specific role in Jesus' life. Jesus' response to him and Mary in the Temple indicates that Jesus' human heart has become so sensitized to the voice of God the Father that Joseph's own role in Jesus' life must shift.

Joseph has always sought to do whatever the Lord asks of him, and now it is time for him to help deepen Jesus' sensitivity to the same voice. Luke's Gospel, after recounting the story of Jesus in the Temple, tells us that Jesus "went down with them and came to Nazareth, and was obedient to them" (Luke 2:51). As mentioned earlier, the English word *obedient* comes from the Latin word that means "listen to." It is time for Joseph to help Jesus listen more deeply to the Father and so become more obedient.

It was the voice of the Lord that led Joseph to ask for Mary's hand in marriage. It was the voice of the Lord that Joseph relied on when he first heard that Mary was pregnant. And it was the voice of the Lord that Joseph needed to hear in Bethlehem when he realized there was no room for them in the inn. On the frightful night when the Holy Family fled to Egypt, it was the Lord's voice that Joseph depended on. Throughout his life, as soon as Joseph was clear about *who* is speaking to him, he immediately surrendered and did what the Lord was asking. Joseph knows the voice of the Lord, and now it is time to teach Jesus about this voice that is deep within his heart.

Let us ask the Holy Spirit to show us Joseph teaching Jesus as a teenager how to recognize the voice of God the Father. The morning tradition of rising early for prayer has become a habit for Jesus, a habit he learned from Joseph. They now rise together, for they enjoy praying in each other's company. Sometimes they go to the hilltops of Nazareth, and other times they stay at home. Joseph is teaching Jesus about silence, contemplation, and the subtleties of the spiritual life. Specifically, Joseph teaches Jesus how to recognize God's voice in the interior movements of his soul.

After they have prayed, Joseph asks Jesus about what he heard and experienced during prayer. These conversations sharpen the teenager's vocabulary and sensitivity to all that is happening within him. Later, as the two of them work together, Joseph is also teaching Jesus how to hear the voice of the Lord in the midst of the activity, busyness, and noise of the workshop.

As we look at the life of Jesus in his public ministry, we see him rising early in the morning to pray. We see that Jesus only wants to do what the Father tells him to do. While Jesus is fully divine, he is also fully human, and it was Joseph's tutelage that helped Jesus grow into the contemplative obedience that defined the rest of his life.

Today's spiritual exercise

Read John 5:19-24. In your prayer, imagine how Joseph's tutelage helps the teenage Jesus learn the ways of praying that he would later embody in his adult life.

_____

_____

_____

_____

_____

_____

_____

_____

_____

_____

_____

_____

_____

_____

_____

Day 27
WISDOM

There are differences between information, knowledge, and wisdom. One may know lots of tidbits and have access to a mass of facts or trivia. But having lots of information does not necessarily mean you know anything substantial.

One may also have lots of knowledge. Whether from formal education or self-study, intellectual formation is often an essential first step to understanding the more essential things in life. However, learning the thoughts of others is just a beginning. Wisdom challenges us to go deeper.

Wisdom can be defined as the quality of having experience, knowledge, and good judgment. Wisdom is when the mind and heart become seasoned by life and by the mystical and incarnational realities surrounding us. Wisdom does not come from just memorizing Scripture. It comes in the refinement of conforming our lives to Scripture. Wisdom requires humility as much as learning. Wisdom guides us so that we do not make mistakes, and it enables us to learn from the mistakes we do make. People who possess wisdom understand life. They know and have experienced suffering. They have matured through their experience and gained an understanding of what life means.

God the Father chose Joseph to teach Jesus about life. Luke tells us that in Nazareth, Jesus "increased in wisdom and in stature" (Luke 2:52). Surely many people helped Jesus advance in wisdom. But we can be confident that Joseph was one of those essential wisdom figures for Jesus.

Let us ask the Holy Spirit to reveal to us how Joseph helped Jesus advance in wisdom. Let us imagine the moments when Jesus asked Joseph about the story of Joseph's life. Imagine the impact on Jesus as Joseph shared all the struggles of the years we read about in the first chapters of Matthew and Luke. As Joseph honestly responds to Jesus about his own personal struggles, Jesus is reminded that life does not always meet our expectations.

There is also something about suffering that imparts wisdom in ways few other things can. Whether in his stories about the flight to Egypt and the massacre of the Holy Innocents or by his example showing Jesus how to endure the brutal Roman occupation, Joseph has been teaching Jesus about suffering and so helping him gain wisdom from the daily realities of life.

Joseph's teaching and example would have enabled Jesus to appreciate the more subtle aspects of wisdom, such as how to be patient, how to wait, and how to ask questions instead of giving answers. Joseph would also have taught Jesus the arts of conversation and storytelling, how to use concrete and natural images to explain complex theological realities. These are tools often used by people who appreciate wisdom. We can imagine Joseph sharing stories and parables with Jesus as a means of helping Jesus advance in wisdom.

What we know is that Jesus advanced in wisdom, and Joseph was essential to that process.

Today's spiritual exercise

Read Proverbs 3:13-18. In your prayer, imagine how Joseph's tutelage helped the teenage Jesus advance in wisdom.

_____

_____

_____

_____

_____

_____

_____

_____

_____

_____

_____

Day 28
WORKER

Every May 1, the Catholic Church celebrates the feast day of St. Joseph the Worker. As we continue to consider life in Nazareth and what Jesus would have learned there, we see that hard work would have been an essential virtue that Joseph fostered within Jesus.

It wasn't just *that* Joseph worked but *how* Joseph worked. Let us imagine Joseph beginning each project with prayer and pausing periodically throughout his work to ask God for help and thank God for blessings. Joseph worked with God, in rhythm with the movement of God. Work was not something that Joseph did on behalf of God, but rather something that Joseph did in harmony with God.

Let us ask the Holy Spirit to help us imagine how Joseph teaches Jesus to pay attention to the small details in the way he works. As a carpenter, Joseph has to pay attention to details. This virtue is not just helpful in the craft of building but also essential in life. Joseph also pays attention to the details of his marriage—to Mary's disposition and body language, the precise things that support her and help her feel safe and secure. He notices the things she likes and what makes her happy.

Joseph's work ethic also teaches Jesus how to complete a job and how to give when you think you have nothing left to give. Indeed, there are days when Joseph may not feel like working but chooses to do so anyway. Indeed, there are days when Joseph wants to be doing other things but decides to stay with his work instead.

These gifts would have been a part of what Jesus learned about life by working alongside Joseph.

Today's spiritual exercise

Read Psalm 90:14-17. Now imagine that you are with Joseph and Jesus in the workshop. Imagine that you are with them preparing wooden staves for the celebration of Passover. The instructions of Exodus 12 say that a Passover lamb had to be roasted before it was consumed, and first-century historians tell us that the roasting required two staves for each sacrificed lamb. The first staff ran horizontally across the open front legs, and the second staff ran vertically from the neck to the back legs, with the legs tied together at the bottom. Thus, according to ancient Passover custom, the lambs were roasted in cruciform.

Joseph has been asked to bring two thousand staves to Jerusalem for the upcoming Passover. He and Jesus are working together, planing the wood into small staves. As they work, Joseph and the teenage Jesus talk about Passover, the sacrificial lambs, and how the Lord set Israel free from slavery. There is a sacred silence as Jesus holds the staves of wood. Joseph watches Jesus staring at the wood that will hold these "crucified" Passover lambs. The words of Matthew 1 return to Joseph's mind:

"You shall call his name Jesus, for he will save his people from their sins." Joseph ponders these words anew as he beholds Jesus.

_____

_____

_____

_____

_____

_____

_____

_____

_____

_____

_____

_____

_____

_____

_____

Day 29
DEATH

Scripture does not tell us when Joseph died, but the absence of any mention of him during Jesus' public ministry leads us to believe that Joseph's death preceded Jesus' baptism at the beginning of his public ministry. Let us ask the Holy Spirit to help us enter into a most sacred scene, the death of Joseph.

Joseph's life is nearing its end. He has been tired for a few weeks and is bedridden now. He doesn't seem to be suffering with a specific illness; it is more that his life has simply run its course. He has become quieter of late, more contemplative and more reflective. Both Mary and Jesus have noticed his deepening silence, and it seems as if all three have intuited the twilight of his life and his impending death.

Today, Mary sat at his bedside for hours. They reminisced about how they met, the early years in Bethlehem and Egypt, and the joys they have experienced in Nazareth in this very house. Joseph thanked Mary for her holiness and consecration, reminding Mary that her mere presence always made Joseph want to be a better man.

Now it is sunset. The day has been beautiful, but tonight's sunset is magnificent. Mary and Joseph often walked to the hilltops of Nazareth to enjoy the magnificent sunsets. Jesus also has hundreds of sacred memories of those hilltop sunsets, where some of his best conversations with Joseph took place. Joseph has asked for one last thing: Would they lift his head so he can see the sunset through the window?

Mary raises his head. She caresses Joseph's hair and gently kisses his hand as she thanks Joseph for being such a safe place for her purity. She reminds Joseph that she has never had to question his motives or worry about his commitment to listening to God. She has always cherished these things about him, and in the sacredness of this moment she thanks Joseph specifically for these gifts.

This night there is more that they say to each other. There is quiet laughter and more tears and more silence and more gratitude.

At the end of their conversation, Joseph asks Mary if she remembers what they said to each other the very first night they moved into this home. Mary smiles. Joseph says to her again tonight, "He who finds a wife finds a good thing, and obtains favor from the LORD" (Proverbs 18:22). Mary places her hand on his heart, looks deep into his eyes, and says now as she did then, "Truly God is good to the upright, to those who are pure in heart" (Psalm 73:1).

Jesus has also had tender moments with Joseph throughout this day. Now Joseph asks Jesus to make sure that he cares for Mary. Jesus laughs with tenderness as he says to Joseph, "I will, but no mere man can love her the way you do." Joseph's eyes fill with tears. Soon his eyes close and there is now only silence in the house.

The sun has set, and the dark of night has also entered the house of the Holy Family. Joseph's breathing has slowed. As Mary holds his hand, Jesus kneels on his other side. With tenderness, Jesus whispers to Joseph, "I will come and get you." Joseph smiles, squeezes Mary's hand, and takes his final breath.

Today's spiritual exercise

Enter into today's meditation as if you were there. Be with Joseph. Be with Mary. Be with Jesus. Be with the Holy Family in the scene as it unfolds.

_____

_____

_____

_____

_____

_____

_____

_____

_____

_____

Day 30
BEGIN

The day has come. It has been a day that Mary has anticipated for thirty years, as Jesus leaves their home in Nazareth to begin his public ministry. Let us ask the Holy Spirit to help us imagine all that unfolds today.

Mary's experience with Jesus at the wedding in Cana showed her that the time had come for him to begin his ministry. And reports have reached Nazareth that John is baptizing in the Jordan. Just last night, when Mary first heard that John was baptizing, she remembered her visit to Elizabeth many years before, and how John stirred in the womb of his mother when Mary entered the room that day.

Today's sunrise is beautiful, almost as if something new is dawning. As Mary wakes and begins her morning routine, she can tell that Jesus is ready. In what seems like a timeless silence, Mary walks with Jesus to the door. She places both her hands on the side of his cheeks and looks at him earnestly, quoting the prophet Isaiah: "Behold, I am doing a new thing; now it springs forth, do you not perceive it?" (Isaiah 43:19). Jesus kisses his mother's forehead and quotes Isaiah back to her, smiling: "You are precious in my eyes, and honored, and I love you" (Isaiah 43:4).

Jesus speaks a prayer of blessing over his mother and takes his first steps out the door. As he walks away, she closes it gently behind him and goes to a window to watch him. When she can no longer see him, she pauses for a moment to reflect, remembering all that has happened in this house. She thinks of Joseph, and she smiles when she considers how proud he would be this day.

Moved with deep emotion, Mary longs for Joseph as a wife longs for her husband after his death. Something about this day's significance makes Mary want to share it with him. His tomb is less than half a mile from the house, and Mary decides that she would like to go there now.

As Mary approaches Joseph's tomb, her heart is brimming with emotion. But what she sees there makes her hold back, for she is not the only one who felt the need to visit Joseph today. She sees Jesus kneeling before the tomb, his hands and his cheek pressed against its stone entrance. With tears in his eyes, Jesus turns to his mother and says the very words that Mary spoke to Joseph every night: "Truly God is good to the upright, to those who are pure in heart" (Psalm 73:1).

They remain there together in silence for a while. Then Mary takes Jesus' hand as he stands. Turning his head a last time to look at Joseph's tomb, Jesus whispers again, "I will come and get you."

With the Jordan River in front of him, Jesus begins to move into the sunlight and into his public ministry. Seeing so many of the attributes of Joseph in Jesus, Mary watches her son walking in the distance and quietly repeats, "Truly God is good to the upright, to those who are pure in heart."

Today's spiritual exercise

Enter into today's meditation as if you were there in the scene. Be with Mary. Be with Jesus. Be with them in the scene as it unfolds.

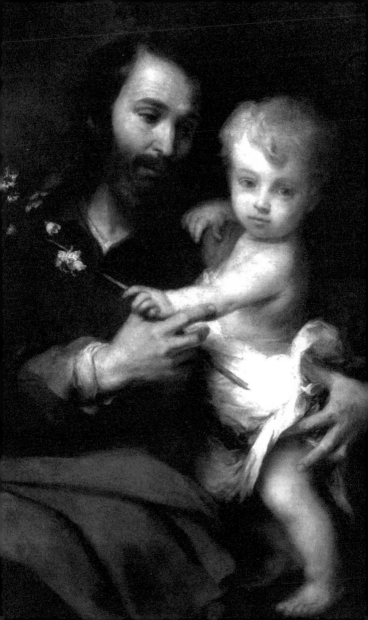

CONCLUSION

Through these meditations, St. Joseph has invited us to encounter his heart. May I ask you today to invite him into your heart? It is my prayer that you now have a personal understanding of Joseph as the profound man he was and the saint he is. I pray that at the end of this journey you can appreciate why God the Father chose this particular man to reveal masculinity and fatherhood to Jesus.

As our journey concludes, may I offer a few final thoughts.

First, ask Joseph to intercede for you every day.

Second, to the men who are reading: I don't know who your model for manhood, marriage, or fatherhood has been. But if God himself hand-picked Joseph, I venture that there is no one better. If we men are not striving to be like Joseph, why not?

Finally, for everyone who has read these meditations, I encourage you to revisit the ones that spoke to your heart most personally. Don't be afraid to reread the meditations and pray with them periodically throughout the year—for each time we pray with St. Joseph, there will always be something new and fresh awaiting us.

NOTES

1   Benedict XVI, *Jesus of Nazareth: The Infancy Narratives* (New York: Image, 2012), 67.

2   Benedict XVI, 94, 97.

3   Benedict XVI, 97.

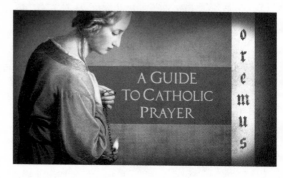